Published in 2016 by Hardie Grant Books

Hardie Grant Books (Melbourne)
Building 1, 658 Church Street
Richmond, Victoria 3121

Hardie Grant Books (London)
5th & 6th Floors
52–54 Southwark Street
London SE1 1UN

hardiegrantbooks.com

A Cataloguing-in-Publication entry is available from the catalogue of the
National Library of Australia at www.nla.gov.au

The World According to Trump
ISBN 978 1 74379 210 0

Cover design by Oslo Davis
Text design by Mark Campbell
Typeset in Bodoni by Andy Warren

Printed and bound in China by 1010 Printing International Limited

The
World
According
to
Trump

Humble words from the man who would be king, president, ruler of the world …

Illustrations by Oslo Davis

hardie grant books

INTRODUCTION

'I don't put on any airs,' Donald J Trump once told a journalist, from behind his 'one-hundred per cent mahogany' desk. Half the size of a squash court, and brightened up with a stuffed bald eagle, this desk sits amid shelves full of golf trophies and dozens of 'important awards' with framed magazine covers all over the walls (no prizes for guessing who's on them). From the windows, one can see Central Park – but the real spectacle is the lobby below: gold-plated, pink-marbled and perfumed, it contains chandeliers and a sixty-foot waterfall, plus guards in red jackets and furry black hats.

The building's name, of course, is Trump Tower. As you can see from the huge sign outside.

Could it be that Donald does actually put on airs? That his light isn't completely hidden under a bushel? After all, ever since he burst onto the scene in a blaze of blondes, boasts and stunningly bad hair, the real estate mogul has given us the Trump World Tower and the Trump Castle. Plus Trump Palace, and a few Trump Hotels. Then there's the Trump Regency and the various Trump Taj Mahals, together with Trump Park Avenue and several Trump Plazas.

For a full picture of this man's personality, we should probably also factor in the Trump Marina and the seven Trump golf clubs, plus the Trump Winery and the many Trump restaurants. Americans can also dress like Donald, courtesy of the Donald J Trump Signature Collection, or smell like him, thanks to Donald Trump: The Fragrance.

And for just a few more dollars, they can think like him, too. On the shelves at the Trump Store, there sit no fewer than seventeen 'personally written' books by Donald Trump on the subject of Trump. They have titles like *Trump: The Way to the Top* and *Trump: Think Like a Champion*. Resplendent with photos, of course.

And then there is Donald's latest volume, *Crippled America*, which boasts a sixteen-page 'About the Author' section mostly concerned with what he plans to do once he lives in the White House.

Whether 'President Trump' ever becomes a reality is not really the question, but just *how* he got so far is. Perhaps the answer is in this modest tome, *The World According to Trump*, which contains the decidedly immodest words of Donald Trump and reveals all you ever wanted to know about the man, and probably a great deal more.

'I was always very much accepted by my father. He adored Donald Trump.'

The son of Friedrich Drumpf, a German immigrant, Frederick Trump built tens of thousands of affordable houses in the low-income areas of Brooklyn and Queens. He had five children, a thriving real estate company and around $400 million at the time of his death.

'When I look at myself in the first grade and I look at myself now, I'm basically the same. The temperament is not that different.'

According to his brother Robert, 'Donald was the child who would throw the cake at the birthday parties.'

'I felt like I was in the military in a true sense.'

Trump was sent to military school at the age of fourteen. 'He thought he was Mr America and the world revolved around him,' says his former instructor, Colonel Dobias.

'I went to the Wharton School of Business. I'm, like, a really smart person. I was a really good student at the best school in the country.'

Trump did not graduate with honours of any kind, even though 'just about every profile ever written about him states that he graduated first in his class'.

'The first thing I did when I got out of college was to analyse the current economic climate and think about just what business I wanted to go into.'

The second thing he did was go into his father's business. 'My whole life really has been a 'no' and I fought through it. It has not been easy for me, it has not been easy for me … My father gave me a small loan of $1 million.'

*'I'm a builder; I know how to build.
Nobody can build like I can build.'*

Trump's first big project, Trump Tower, was built
with concrete from a company owned by 'Fat Tony'
Salerno and 'Big Paul' Castellano, the heads of the
Genovese and Gambino crime families.

'There is no one my age who has accomplished more. Everyone can't be the best.'

Trump reflecting on his achievements in 1987, at the age of 41.

'Oftentimes when I was sleeping with one of the top women in the world, I would say to myself, thinking about me as a boy from Queens, "Can you believe what I am getting?"'

He also accomplished a lot in the bedroom, according to *Think Big: Make it happen in business and life.*

'I would never buy Ivana any decent jewels or pictures. Why give her negotiable assets?'

On his first marriage, to fashion model
Ivana Trump.

It ended a year later.

'I only have one regret in the women department – that I never had the opportunity to court Lady Diana Spencer.'

According to UK TV presenter Selina Scott, Donald did 'court' her. After Diana and Charles divorced in 1996, Trump 'bombarded Diana at Kensington Palace with massive bouquets of flowers, each worth hundreds of pounds,' Scott wrote in the *Sunday Times*. 'What am I going to do?' the princess supposedly asked Scott. 'He gives me the creeps.'

'I was bored when she was walking down the aisle. I kept thinking: "What the hell am I doing here?" I was so deep into my business stuff. I couldn't think of anything else.'

On the promising start to his second marriage in 1993, which also ended in a nasty divorce.

'It's certainly not groundbreaking news that the early victories by the women on The Apprentice *were, to a very large extent, dependent on their sex appeal.'*

On the reality show he starred in and co-produced.

'They didn't cut ties with me, I cut ties with them.'

On NBC's decision to ditch *The Apprentice.*

'I'm the most successful person to ever run for the presidency, by far ... We will have so much winning if I get elected that you may get bored with winning.'

On his bid for the presidency.

*'I win, I win, I always win. In the end,
I always win. Whether it's in
golf, whether it's in tennis, whether it's
in life, I just always win.'*

A fairly typical excerpt from *Trump Nation: The art
of being Donald.*

'Sorry losers and haters, but my IQ is one of the highest – and you all know it!'

A 2013 tweet to all the haters on Twitter.

'People love me. And you know what,
I have been very successful.
Everybody loves me.'

From a TV interview. Specific people who 'love'
Donald Trump (according to Donald Trump)
include 'the blacks', 'beautiful women', 'Latinos',
'evangelicals', 'poor people', 'bankers', 'veterans',
'Hollywood people', 'Tea Party activists' and
'the middle class'.

'I was always the best athlete.'

On his many golf championships, in an interview in *The Atlantic*. The same article also quotes a source that calls him 'the most rampant cheater'.

'I'm intelligent. Some people would say I'm very, very, very intelligent.'

Explaining in a *Fortune* magazine interview in 2000 why it is that he 'could be the first presidential candidate to run and make money on it'.

'I have a great temperament. My temperament is very good, very calm.'

Trump's biographers have accused him of 'bullying and harassment' and of having a 'ferocious temper'.

'Many are saying I'm the best 140-character writer in the world.'

On Twitter.

'I believe in winning. I'm very good at winning.'

From a 2015 *Bloomberg* interview.

'Part of the beauty of me is that I'm very rich.'

On *Good Morning America*, explaining why he's good for America.

*'I'm worth much more
than $10 billion.'*

As of 2015, according to *Bloomberg Business* and
Forbes respectively, he's actually worth somewhere
between $2.9 billion and $4.5 billion. 'Donald
has never had the net worth he claimed,' says
one acquaintance.

'The reason my hair looks so neat all the time is because I don't have to deal with the elements very often. I live in the building where I work. I take an elevator from my bedroom to my office. The rest of the time, I'm either in my stretch limousine, my private jet, my helicopter, or my private club in Palm Beach, Florida … If I happen to be outside, I'm probably on one of my golf courses, where I protect my hair from overexposure by wearing a golf hat.'

Relating to the common man during an interview in 2004.

'I've never had any trouble in bed ...'

From *Trump: Surviving at the Top*. 'I was out four or five nights a week,' he wrote elsewhere of his eighties heyday, 'usually with a different woman each time.'

*'I have one of the greatest
memories of all time.'*

Apropos of nothing, to *The Hollywood Reporter*.

'Somebody really, really handsome.'

On who should play him in an HBO movie.

*'I can be a very elegant,
highly refined person.'*

Being modest.

'While I can't honestly say I need an 80-foot living room, I get a kick out of having one.'

On his home.

'I show [my] apartment to very few people. Presidents. Kings.'

A passing comment on *The Apprentice*,
made from inside his apartment.

*'It's bigger than Air Force One,
which is a step down from this in every
way. Rolls-Royce engines; seats 43.
Didja know it was featured on the
Discovery Channel as the world's most
luxurious jetliner?'*

On his private jet, which has never been on
the Discovery Channel and is smaller than
Air Force One.

'It turned out to be, probably, by everybody's count, the biggest-selling business book of all time. There's never been a business book that's sold like Trump: The Art of the Deal.*'*

Actually, there have been quite a few
that sold more.

'You have to treat 'em like shit.'

On his approach to women, according to a 1992 article in *New York* magazine.

'The fact is, I don't like publicity.
I absolutely hate doing interviews.'

From a 1987 interview.

'My favourite part [of Pulp Fiction*]*
is when Sam has his gun out in the
diner and he tells the guy to tell his
girlfriend to shut up. "Tell that bitch
to be cool. Say: 'Bitch, be cool.'"
I love those lines.'

On cinema.

'I remember attending a magnificent dinner being given by one of the most admired people in the world. I was seated next to a lady of great social pedigree and wealth … All of a sudden I felt her hand on my knee, then on my leg. She started petting me in all different ways. "Donald," she said, "I don't care. I just don't care. I have to have you, and I have to have you now."'

An anecdote from *Trump: The Art of the Comeback*.

'*All of the women on* The Apprentice *flirted with me – consciously or unconsciously. That's to be expected.*'

An excerpt from *How to Get Rich*.

'You dropped to your knees? That must be a pretty picture, you dropping to your knees.'

To a female contestant on *The Apprentice*.

'I think the only difference between me and the other candidates is that I'm more honest and my women are more beautiful.'

On what sets him apart.

*'There's nothing I love
more than women.'*

However, a 2015 news poll suggested that
62 per cent of female voters held an unfavourable
view of Trump.

'She's not giving me 100 per cent. She's giving me 84 per cent, and 16 per cent is going towards taking care of children.'

His thoughts on hiring working mothers.

'I've known Paris Hilton from the time she was twelve. Her parents are friends of mine, and, you know, the first time I saw her, she walked into the room and I said, "Who the hell is that?" … Well, at twelve, I wasn't interested. I've never been into that.'

Just in case you were wondering.

'Nobody cares about the talent. There's only one talent you care about, and that's the look talent. You don't give a shit if a girl can play a violin like the greatest violinist in the world. You want to know: what does she look like.'

On beauty pageants. He has owned part or all of Miss Universe, Miss USA and Miss Teen USA since 1996.

'I am the least racist person there is. And I think most people that know me would tell you that. I am the least racist.'

Responding to criticism after a 2011 press conference in which he said that President Obama should 'get off his basketball court' and that a black reporter 'must be a big Obama fan'.

*'Laziness is a trait in blacks ...
Black [bankers] counting my money!
I hate it. The only kind of people
I want counting my money are little
short guys that wear yarmulkes
every day.'*

A quote attributed to Trump by a former colleague in a 'tell-all book'. Trump later called the book 'probably true'.

'I understand the Chinese mind.'

On how, when it comes to trade deals, Trump
manages to 'beat China all the time'.

*'This is a country where we speak
English, not Spanish.'*

On America's 40 million Spanish speakers.

'The US has become a dumping ground for everybody else's problems … When Mexico sends its people, they're not sending their best. They're sending people that have lots of problems … they're bringing drugs, they're bringing crime. They're rapists. And some, I assume, are good people.'

On the need for a 3200-kilometre wall between the US and Mexico.

'I will build a great wall – and nobody builds walls better than me, believe me – and I'll build them very inexpensively. I will build a great, great wall on our southern border, and I will make Mexico pay for that wall. Mark my words.'

On his immigration policy.

'For a man to be successful he needs support at home, just like my father had from my mother, not someone who is always griping and bitching. When a man has to endure a woman who is not supportive and complains constantly about his not being home enough or not being attentive enough, he will not be very successful unless he is able to cut the cord.'

On marital bliss.

'I think that putting a wife to work is a very dangerous thing. There was a great softness to Ivana, and she still has that softness, but during this period of time, she became an executive, not a wife ... You know, I don't want to sound too much like a chauvinist, but when I come home and dinner's not ready, I'll go through the roof, okay?'

On the short and traumatic period in which his first wife had her own life.

*'She really has become a monster …
I mean monster in the most
positive way.'*

On his second wife during her pregnancy.

'I am a nice person. People that know me like me. Does my family like me? I think so.'

On family.

'I want five children, like in my own family, because with five, then I will know that one will be guaranteed to turn out like me.'

From a 1990 profile in *Vanity Fair*. Trump does now have five children – including Donald Trump, Jr.

'The hardest thing for me about raising kids has been finding the time. I know friends who leave their business so they can spend more time with their children, and I say, "Gimme a break!"'

On fatherhood.

'She does have a very nice figure. I've said if Ivanka weren't my daughter, perhaps I'd be dating her.'

On how he would react if his daughter posed for *Playboy*.

'She's got the best body.'

On his daughter.

'Yeah, she's really something, and what a beauty, that one. If I weren't happily married and, ya know, her father …'

Still on his daughter.

'They're great marksmen, great shots,
they love it.'

Defending his sons after they were photographed
in Africa alongside dead leopards and elephants.

'Not teaching your kids about money is like not caring whether they eat.'

On parenting.

'Don't let the brevity of these passages prevent you from savouring the profundity of the advice you are about to receive.'

From the introduction to *How to Get Rich*.

'Show me someone without an ego, and I'll show you a loser.'

In response to the suggestion that he didn't need to put the word 'Trump' in huge, golden letters on everything he builds or owns.

'I think if this country gets any kinder or gentler, it's literally going to cease to exist.'

On President-elect Bush's call for a kinder, gentler nation in 1990.

'I definitely would apologise if I were wrong on something.'

On why the word 'sorry' rarely exits his mouth.

'What did these geniuses expect when they put men and women together?'

On sexual harassment and sexual assault in the military.

'If you're interested in "balancing" work and pleasure, stop trying to balance them. Instead make your work more pleasurable.'

On how 'success requires work seven days a week'.

'If somebody hits you, hit back ten times harder.'

Trump on getting 'even'. Some of the people
he's sued over the years include a Native American
tribe, a small card shop, both of his ex-wives,
the people of Scotland and the state of New York.

'People that go to faraway places to help out are great – but must suffer the consequences.'

On why people who went to Africa to help with the Ebola crisis should stay there, possibly forever.

*'The concept of global warming
was created by and for the Chinese
in order to make US manufacturing
non-competitive.'*

On climate science.

*'One thing I have learned: there
is high maintenance. There is low
maintenance. I want no maintenance.'*

On the ideal relationship.

'Remember, new "environment friendly" light bulbs can cause cancer. Be careful – the idiots who came up with this stuff don't care.'

On energy efficiency.

'My fingers are long and beautiful, as, it has been well documented, are various other parts of my body.'

In response to *Spy* magazine calling him a 'short-fingered vulgarian' in the eighties.

'*Something very important, and indeed society-changing, may come out of the Ebola epidemic that will be a very good thing: NO SHAKING HANDS!*'

Much like Howard Hughes, Trump is a long-time germaphobe.

'Who wouldn't take Kate's picture and make lots of money if she does the nude sunbaking thing. Come on, Kate!'

Defending the photographer who snapped a pic of a topless Kate Middleton from a mile away, using a long-range lens.

'One of the key problems today is that politics is such a disgrace. Good people don't go into government.'

On politics.

*'I can look at people and see
what they are.'*

On his powers of perception.

*'Heidi Klum. Sadly,
she's no longer a ten.'*

From a *New York Times* interview.

'*In my opinion, the social scene – in New York, Palm Beach or anywhere else, for that matter – is full of phonies and unattractive people who often have done nothing smarter than inherit somebody else's wealth.*'

According to some calculations, if Trump had never done a day's work in his life, but just put his $40 million inheritance into an index fund, he would be a much richer man today.

'You're disgusting. You're disgusting.'

To a lawyer during a court case when she asked for a medical break to pump breast milk. 'He got up, his face got red, he shook his finger at me … and he ran out of there.'

'Rosie O'Donnell's disgusting both inside and out. You take a look at her, she's a slob. She talks like a truck driver, she doesn't have her facts, she'll say anything that comes to her mind. Her show failed when it was a talk show, the ratings went very, very, very low and very bad, and she got essentially thrown off television. I mean she's basically a disaster.'

Coping well after the TV host said he was 'not a self-made man'.

'A bunch of major jerks.'

On the Rolling Stones after they refused to appear
alongside him at a press conference to advertise an
upcoming show at Trump Plaza

'While Bette Midler is an extremely unattractive woman, I refuse to say that because I always insist on being politically correct.'

Diplomatically responding to a complaint from the actress that some of his buildings had 'ruined New York'.

'Look at that face! Would anyone vote for that? Can you imagine that, the face of our next president.'

More or less his only observation to date about fellow Republican presidential candidate Carly Fiorina.

'*If Hillary Clinton can't satisfy her husband what makes her think she can satisfy America?*'

A tweet Donald quickly deleted – but not quite quickly enough.

'Cher is somewhat of a loser. She's lonely. She's unhappy. She's very miserable.'

Striking back after the singer described him as a 'loudmouth', a 'racist cretin' and 'an arrogant and obnoxious asshole with an ego the size of Texas'.

'He is not a war hero ... He is a war hero because he was captured. I like people who weren't captured, OK?'

On Senator John McCain, a man who was subjected to torture, disease, broken bones and beatings as a POW for more than five years. Trump, in contrast, spent the Vietnam War in New York.

'A spoiled brat without a properly functioning brain.'

On the 'truly weird' Senator Rand Paul.

'Arianna Huffington is unattractive both inside and out. I fully understand why her former husband left her for a man – he made a good decision.'

Trump has never quite forgiven the *Huffington Post* founder for announcing that her site would feature his presidential campaign in its entertainment pages, rather than the politics section.

'He put on glasses so people think he's smart ... People can see through that.'

On (the admittedly dopey) Texas Republican Rick Perry.

'I really understand beauty. And I will tell you, she's not – I do own Miss Universe. I do own Miss USA. I mean, I own a lot of different things. I do understand beauty, and she's not.'

On Angelina Jolie.

'While Jon Stewart is a joke, not very bright and totally overrated, some losers and haters will miss him and his dumb clown humour. Too bad!'

Donald never liked the way the *Daily Show* host nicknamed him 'Fuckface von Clownstick'.

'You could see there was blood coming out of her eyes. Blood coming out of her wherever.'

Donald wasn't happy when a 'bimbo' journalist accused him of insulting women by calling them 'pigs, dogs, slobs and disgusting animals'.

'To EVERYONE, including all haters and losers, HAPPY NEW YEAR. Work hard, be smart and always remember, WINNING TAKES CARE OF EVERYTHING.'

On his life philosophy.